# MINIATURES

# MINIATURES

*poems*

Meredith Cole

*For Beatrice,*
*Thank you for all the lovely*
*haircuts.*
*Best wishes,*
*Meredith*

MHP

Marsh Hawk Press
*East Rockaway, NY • 2012*

12 13 14 15 16   7 6 5 4 3 2 1   First Edition

Marsh Hawk Press books are published by Poetry Mailing List, Inc.,
a not-for-profit corporation under section 501 (c) 3
United States Internal Revenue Code.

Cover art: Darren Waterston
*Fugue*, 2007,  40.5 x 28.5 inches,
pigment print on innova paper, edition of 20.

Art photo credit: Gallery 16, San Francisco.

Author photo: Andrew Drake.

Cover and interior design by Claudia Carlson.
The text is set in Adobe Jenson Pro Light and the display in Dax.

Library of Congress Cataloging-in-Publication Data

Miniatures : poems / by Meredith Cole. -- 1st ed.
p. cm.
ISBN-13: 978-0-9846353-5-1 (pbk.)
ISBN-10: 0-9846353-5-1 (pbk.)

Marsh Hawk Press
P.O. Box 206, East Rockaway, N.Y. 11518-0206
www.marshhawkpress.org

*for Chris*

## ACKNOWLEDGMENTS

Some of these poems were previously published in the following journals: *Cream City Review, Field, Poetry, The Iowa Review,* and *The Seattle Review.* Thank you to Jessica Johnson.

Thank you to my parents, Robert and Charlotte Cole, and to Melissa Poort, Adam Cole and Ryan Cole.

Last, my love and thanks to Chris and Wade Lewis.

# CONTENTS

# MINIATURES

*In autumn fields, pine crickets call,*
*"We wait, we wait."*
*If I go out to meet them, I will answer,*
*"Is it me? Am I the one?"*

—ANONYMOUS

# SEVEN VEILS

We passed a truck
loaded with logs on the narrow road.
Our driver tried teaching us Japanese as we gunned it,
motioning to blue-green butterflies drifting by.
*Cho cho*, he said and smiled.
We crested the hilltop,
the smell of creosote and pavement
burning a path as rain fell
through low-drifting clouds and smoke billows—
the other truck, jackknifed, crushed
against the barrier, had fallen
to the green below. Our driver
grunted, kept driving
as people smoked
on the roadside motioning for help.
Smoke made the sunset red,
layering pink like seven veils,
a strange sunset over the valley.
Seven dead, though we didn't know,
just tourists in a strange land,
passing darkened towns,
beautiful girls, dead ends,
and misty passes in which monkeys howled.
By moonlight, we didn't know
what we were driving through
as a pygmy owl called once in the darkness
and bit a butterfly in two.

## DAISIES

Meredith and her ex-boyfriend walked all the way
to Uwajima. You have never been to Japan,
you don't know how far that is,
and how the sky was dull orange with white clouds.
Meredith said she was unhappy
and that the fortune-teller read her death in the cards.
The ex-boyfriend asked how that could be true
and Meredith tried to express how the sadness was huge,
as huge as the Board of Education building
in Uwajima. She said she was sad even when looking
at a daisy and then the ex-boyfriend knew.
For some time he carried her, you who
have never been to Japan don't know how far
that is, and the little daisies winked closed for the night,
the squid boats lit up the dark bay with their green lights,
and sometimes a car pulled over and the person inside
asked if they needed a ride, and Meredith leaned
against her ex-boyfriend's back and he answered,
No, no, we're all right, politely, very politely,
as people will in rural Japan.

# BEAUTY, WISDOM, LUCK

The saleswoman said,
This jade is nice for children.
As she grows, the jade darkens
until it becomes as full of life
as its owner. Hush Misato,
Misato's mother said,
Grandma didn't mean
to say those things.
But Misato knew she did.
Here, Grandma said,
go ahead, take beauty. Take it,
what do I need beauty for, at my age.
You'd have to dig it up later anyway
and that wouldn't be so pretty.
Misato didn't want beauty anymore
and they bought her wisdom
against the mother's better judgment.
Misato took the furthest seat away,
and Grandma turned her painted face
to look out at downtown traffic.
Luck shone against her chest
like a flash
from a greener, more troubled country.

# THE CHILDREN DREAM OF A WHALE SET FREE

### 1.

*It is dark here and wild.*
*Many bodies die.*

The ocean floor slick with kelp
collects the large shadows.

### 2.

There is a cove hollowed of ice
forming since its own reflection.
The kelp moves in cold groves
in the white reflections.

### 3.

The hum. A humming shape deep as echo
has worn a hole in the echoed sea,

a grooved watermark, a casing
like the sphere in air a flower carves.

The opening blooms
under a soft, dark blanket of sleep.

### 4.

Look at all the shapes firm as rocks
beneath a changing sea,
but this is not one—a shadow slipped past

as of a night with sliding stars,
or fallen snow, white on the sea.

# RELATIONSHIPS

Let's have a long boring talk about our relationship
he said on the local that sped through the foreign town
toward a world famous hot spring. I was thinking
he said about Buddha and how I've obsessed
over his teachings but now I realize
Buddha was wrong to leave his wife and kids
to travel to foreign lands.
The local we rode was identical in fact
to trains destroyed by atomic weapons in the second
world war. The rings
knocked together overhead. I wanted to get drunk
in the rain with red flowers falling over me.
I wanted to be as the poets say
enflamed. Tiny parking lots rushed past
red flowers blooming here and there.
In each flower, the rain.
In each cup of water existed the future
conversation and its devastating consequences.

## AN OLD CASTLE

Her boyfriend said, Let's climb to that castle
and they did but then he didn't want to see the castle
he only wanted to ask her why she'd slept with another man
he wanted to know again and again. She looked
at the wild irises near the white castle.
She assumed they were wild. They blew around
it seemed their stalks might snap with the weight
of the heavy heads. When you want to avoid an argument
the boyfriend said, you always look at flowers.
But you wanted to come to this place
she said. You drove me to a place
where there isn't much to see so I look at the wild irises.
The wild irises actually were wild the girl was right for once
the irises went on making more
irises for hundreds of years after in golds and blues and no one
knew the place of their beginnings as the irises bent and bent
and never once betrayed her secret heart.

# TIDE POOLS

Down the carved sandbank toward camp,
      I could only carry the light sacks,

while you hefted the heaviest pack, pumped water
from a dried-up creek, lit the fire, set the tent.

You eased me from my coat
      and we shed our under things
and alternately zipped our silk cocoons.

Fires lit along the beach look like fires down
in Mexico, you said, as they stretch out

and unknown faces play with darkness
and the strange red firelight. I said, the earth
would kill us if it could, if I could

not make it over the pass of white sand
blown hither and thither, everything disarmingly
      simple, then you should leave me there to die

as the weak were always left behind in days
gone by. Now the night began to send
      its deepest colors and the ocean moved.
I saw faces down the beach illuminated

by fire, and another white face looked down
to see us all,

all the lives at once displayed,
      as under the deepening, darkening night,
the separate campfires swayed.

## OUR FAMILY NAME:
*Woman Praying in the Temple*

Melissa, do they need to know
we are half-Japanese,
that your cheek, glittering
with bronzer, seemed to slip
half-gone from me already?
This is the city
of our great-grandmother's birth.
You watched the old woman bend
over the grate and bend again
to peer at a thick black butterfly.
You pointed out the image
to me as funny.
Somehow you always see
or were you turned
just that once away from me?
Bridges from the 50s
were fragile in the far-off,
I almost broke one staring too long.
This is Hiroshima
even the sparrows in park trees say:
Go ahead, outlive the trap of your name.

# SPACE NEEDLE

When the man took his youngest son, his namesake,
to the Space Needle to look out on a city they knew
nothing about, the boy saw Lake Union and sailboats
drifting so faintly they stilled as if a camera took them,
and clinging to the ropes, large men the boy could crush
merely by thinking it inside this sharp needle threaded
with clouds. The boy thought he and his father
would pierce Lake Union in their space needle, end up
on the other side, in England, where his much-older father
was born on the sixth day of the sixth month, 1906, and later,
when the boy did the work of his father, in an office overlooking
Lake Union, he was surprised that the needle returned one day,
without ever injuring the giant fingers of memory.

# O-BON

She quickly pedaled her bicycle
through a tunnel wet with moss
to catch the fishermen
pitch a tent strung with lanterns
on a dock by the factory
where they dry tiny fish on aluminum sheets.
At 8pm the sky, lavender,
the temple lanterns lit.
10pm, the ikebana sensei mimed
here and here with each sharp twist
of her thin wrist.
At 10:30pm the girls lit boats
made of popsicle sticks
down the dark river.
This made the dogs bark,
made those red flowers push up,
the flowers they say are made of blood,
and made non-native flowers fall down.
She gathered them
for her grandmother's forgotten charm.
This charm forces the dead alive again.
Hurry, Meredith,
now the rainy season begins.

# TRAVELS IN THE DESERT

We were there once,
having slept in a shivering white tent,
        in a heat dying down,

peeling salt from our arms, and our stiff, oily
        hair on the soft ground.
Through the netted roof were stars.

And deep,
down in the canyon, the water-shaped coves,
and the walls of those coves painted by ancient Pueblo.

They are gone. In the harsh moonlight, pots grown dusty
near a dripping pool, in these cooled cliffs,

pots left behind, and corn in the stone grinders.
Only paintings echo clues, with the wheat-yellow spiral

decoded as "migration" or even, as the line curves
tightly inward or loosely out, "no return."

The imprint
of our tent is gone by now, and the wind
that lifted the netting slowly as we breathed in sleep.

And the marks I found in sand
one morning, while filling a pot with water—

curved in the sand, fine lines of snakes.
Thin, exact to the delicate scaling. Then a smooth tangle,

then straight, the gliding tracks slid out to a distant
bleached juniper, and out,
straight out, as far as I could see.

## AT THE RAINBOW HOTEL

As the family ate breakfast on the wide lanai,
two men in white walked leisurely past,
medical bags in hand. A man was planning
to jump from the 27th floor, they told Meredith's dad—
and why were they walking so slowly,
everyone wondered.
This was a place of wonder:
shops sold coral and miniature orchids,
mother-of-pearl carved into doves.
Meredith wanted a doll
with a coconut for a head. Instead,
they bought her a doll dressed like a hula dancer.
Her faint smile had painted teeth.
Meredith said it was an accident
when she dropped it from the balcony.
It was the last night on Waikiki
and the family walked out in the night
where tiki torches burned over fake grass huts.
A beautiful hula dancer shook her hips
while a sad-looking man strummed his ukulele.
Look, Mom said, She tells a story with her hands.
Meredith loved her mom for saying that.
The hula dancer wore a faint smile,
her hands were first a bird, then
the net to catch the bird. Meredith watched.
Paradise was impressed in her memory
as easily as the machine in the lobby
pressed a tiny hibiscus into a penny.

## MEMENTO

We'd walk five miles for an ice cream,
winding our way up hills,
stopping to talk to an old man on a tractor
who offered us tangelos. We'd walk in the day,
when the sky was blue and the ocean below
sparkling, reliving itself, reliving the day.
And we'd walk at night when we could hear
the stream and feel the swallows rushing by.
And the woman we met most nights
on the way back down to town,
she cut the fruit straight off the tree,
slicing it with a shiny knife
and when we thanked her she would say,
you looked hungry so I fed you.
Though we were never hungry there
and wanted what was bitter and what was sweet,
eating the fruit right from the tip of the blade.

## HOMESICK

I pedaled
my bicycle through town.
The auntie in the rice cake shop
smiled, waved.
Mist grown thick, December.
Sometimes, you know,
I didn't think of you.
Steep steps to the shrine
furred with snow.

## RABBITS

A girl cradled it in her arms,
its fur was soft and gray,
she dropped it
when the boys yelled, "Now!"
The feeble retriever gave chase.
They thought it would be fun, it wasn't
what they thought,
it just squatted down low on the field,
wouldn't run
and later the dog's mouth
was full of blood.
Mrs. Hendry kept the hutch up
as punishment until deep December
when the class made paper chains
and the girls played nativity
at recess, in the slight whirling snow.

# HOT AIR BALLOON

When the man walked his daughter across 60 Acres
to look at the hot air balloon that had crashed,
the girl saw how the balloon lashed two ropes across
a man's bare chest. She heard the balloon's dying
dragon's cough, watched its brushed down plumes
heaving less and less in the shadows near the goal posts
where it had scuttled sullenly to lick its wounds.
The girl wondered how a balloon could be so ruined,
and how her father knew to come to this terrible place,
this soccer field filled with doctors and their children,
and later, when she was older, the girl came to know
this place, and places like it, where the giant hand
picks the last good peach of summer
and you grow older and you think nothing of it.

# ORCHIDS

Misato went with her mother
to visit her mother's aunt. The aunt would not
open her door. Auntie! Auntie! Misato's mother called
but still the aunt would not open.
Tiny orchids grew in the driveway's cracks.
They were pink with orange edging, very delicate,
like work some Japanese women might do.
Finally the aunt, who was Japanese, who had lost
her mind, came to the door and opened it, and
a slim line of light from the other side shone through.
I can't come out, they'll eat me, the aunt whispered.
Her hair was greasy and matted to one side
and then a cat mewed. The stench of everything
was unbearable. Later, Misato's mother said,
Those weren't orchids, those were weeds. Those
were orchids, Misato said. I grew up
there, Misato's mother said, I lived with those
crazy people and I know an orchid
when I see one. Misato called back
the orchids to her mind, pink with orange edging
like the delicate work of some Japanese women,
work that takes much care. Orchids seem delicate
but they are hardy, Misato said. It's not
a good enough metaphor, in fact I'm offended, her mother
said and they reached the air-conditioned hotel
which had the usual orchids out front,
those orchids familiar to us.

# WHO WILL KEEP WATCH OVER THE GUARDIANS?

At night, the heat.
> *The non-native flowers went hot in the dirt.*

They shut.
> *Some tossed up their whole lives.*
I saw from the second story

the biggest light.

I touched the side of the train tunnel.
> *You didn't touch the train tunnel.*
No, but I felt the moss, its softness.

There was a shadow burning me.
> *My shadow burned me.*

Mother
> *said, Look, your shadow.*

And you held your mother.
> *No, there wasn't time.*
You held her in your mind.

# MIST CARRIAGE

Mother was unwell,
could not come home that night.
The little girls nested
in a bean bag chair, swallows,
watching through the glass blinds,
for mother to retrieve them.
Grandma and the great-aunt
took them in the green Chevrolet
across town at night. They crossed
a bridge with orange globular lamps
reflected. Past baobabs grown ancient.
At the hospital, doors opened magically,
doors to an enchanted castle.
The girls tried them several times.
Just like the hotels along the beach,
the hospital was crisp inside against
the swaying tropical heat.
Grandma made a charm with feathers,
red feathers fell down,
baobabs groaned outside and moved
their many limbs to catch
whatever tiny thing
floated headlong in the night air.
Meanwhile, the tourists
drank mai tais ocean side.
The only indication, a sudden break
in their relaxing conversations.

# VIEWS OF A JAPANESE TOWN

Even now, clouds are crossing out the sky,
hiding dimensions with stunning simplicity.
Wet fishing nets drop in the far-off sea.
A boy is moving a cow away.
Orange blossoms blacken and break into dirt.
Though we want to know
what the girl is thinking
as she winds nets in the wind,
we can only return to the sky,
which even now, the clouds are erasing.

# DAISIES

One night, Miyamoto-sensei burst through the entry
carrying boughs of flowering branches,
tiny daisies, and the blood-red flowers you find
in August. You must keep in mind it was August,
these things depend on the season
although you have never been to Japan
and you don't know how damn hot it was
and how the air-conditioner was on full-blast.
Miyamoto-sensei said now Meredith would learn
*ikebana* and she would learn it once a week—
Miyamoto-sensei didn't speak English and Meredith
didn't speak much Japanese so they mainly mimed.
Though what do you know, you never bothered
to visit Meredith in Japan, she was lonely
and you were like a dead person to her,
you were no longer written in her address book.
Miyamoto-sensei said that feeling was of number one
importance, the feeling of two small shy daisies
bending toward each other, Meredith accidentally
leaned against Miyamoto-sensei and felt her
sweaty, old woman body, and Miyamoto-sensei
said o.k., o.k. It was August
although how would you know the month
the earth forces the dead
alive again in song in dance in every forgotten art.

## PASSIONFLOWER

The teacher thought they were throwing
her a party!
When she arrived, as it turned out,
she was expected to give young so-and-so
an English lesson.
Young so-and-so revealed sheets
of mimeographed flowers,
she told him all the answers,
what did she care. And there was a flower
she didn't know
and her so-called friends
chanted purple, purple
in Nihon-go, still the teacher didn't know.
They looked it up: passionflower.
I don't know it, she said
and everyone looked put out
like they did when she said
she didn't have a husband.
That night she lay watching shadows
play on her ceiling, listening to
—no, not crickets in the fields—
volunteer fire fighters throwing
beer cans in her yard.
She thought she might see
a passionflower one time in Japan
in a beautiful dreamlike setting.
She hoped she might,
though the one time she did
was much later in Tokyo
behind a prostitute's ear.
The young teacher didn't remember
the word or her longing
to see such a flower
just once before her grip
on the language was gone
for good.

# THE LIGHT BOX

### 1.

I left the museum halfway through,
sickened to see the school uniforms—
white blouse, navy skirt, name stitched
in white on the black patch.
Exactly the same as today.

Or the glass box with something inside:
*chemise of thirteen-year-old girl*
*riding her bike to school.*

Why look at it? Why write it?

*No one was watching, nobody minded.*

### 2.

*Our plot was all rice, no fruit trees.*
*Hard to sing the rice stalks—all of them—in their swaying components.*

The parakeets ate each other in the schoolyard,
they were this mad. To eat each other they half-lost their minds.

Kindergarten classes saw and cried. Children, children all of them—

So it happens that ash treads lightly, threads
the needle of the eye watching.

3.

No one knows yet what a light box can do,
though we try again, we can't help it.

*Beauty is everlasting and dust is for time.*

4.

The birds saw the rice stalks flatten. Some tossed up their whole lives.

The kids are the same.
*The stalks were each different. The wind came*

*from across an ocean.* Mother said, *My kimono pattern*
*was burned into me, the light was that hot,*
*the pattern was beautiful.*

Our family crest *Women Praying in the Temple,*
written on the fabric somewhere.

Why write it?

*Yes, but that was in the design, Misato— that was always*
*in the kimono's design. I can't help it. And now it is always here,*

and now it is always here.

# THE MOON

The moon is small
and isn't white,
wait, is white
and also gray.
Cold its rays. Thin
it stays on brinks
of blacks
we call the sky.
We call it dark
and blue, this
and something else.
It too, is small.
Wide as the holes
we call our eyes.

# HYDRANGEA

They drove quickly on
the Japanese highway, one
time it rained, twice she

passed right through to morning, through summer
when clouds startled her by drifting so

close by. In the fields,
when people waved, she thought she saw
death or worse. Yet once,

hydrangeas, thousands of hydrangeas,
making the black earth green, allowing

pale petals to fall,
follow her, flutter her grief
away, for as the

Japanese say, nothing lasts, look at
this blossom floating on a stream. Though

no one could ever
say which Japanese wrote this,
or the poem in

which such fleeting words are found.

# COPY MACHINE

Alone, the temp made copies.
No one cared to see

a claim she made repeated in green light.
The file room was clean and cold.

Repeated in green light,
the S.S. Clear Cloud's prow in rock,

the sea was clean and cold.
Of this, the temp made copies,

ten of them a claim—a clear-cut case.
No one on land could see.

The top light flashed in cuts of many greens
and the waves made copies.

The heart is clean and cold.
The mind makes copies.

# LILIES

From the basement window, Meredith and the architect
could see green stems of lilies and not the heads.
As the rain fell, Meredith let on
that she had not lost her marbles, though she had.
She did not show the architect her family tree
from whose branches dangled many aerial-rooted
orchids. I see it's beginning to rain, Meredith said
and yes it fell all day. Some days are like this,
the architect said and watched.
Maybe shadows played across her face,
the lilies' shadows, the lilies' heads,
which we, like the architect, can now detect.
The architect stroked her hair, the air
closed the smaller flowers to give them rest,
while the rain fell over the living machine
and the lilies filled with rain. Black beetles scattered,

gold beetles scattered. Clear water filled the cup,
the cup that holds everything and never breaks.

# ANEMONE

How deep and black the ocean grew.

Sometimes a diagonal white line bisected you,
sometimes the sun made you catch fire.

You lived a thousand years
as if you didn't know how to die.

And then, suddenly tides and skies,

and turning inside out, another ocean
in your own deep pocket!

# HANABI *(Fire Flowers, Fireworks)*

You want to know where flowers go?
Some of them don't come to fruit,
Some of them become the night.

Who start as dust and cardboard string,
Who badly outdo the traveling clouds,
Half-alive and people stare at you.

Fall open, fall open, you don't mean to.
Whose tears streak down in dirty trails,
Who boldly blue and beautifully insane,

Who burst their hearts and scream their names.

# PAPER WHITES

On New Year's Eve they became serious
   and bowed at the shrine which ensures much happiness,
in other words, fertility. She wanted

to like her ex-boyfriend and for him to tolerate her,
   so they walked in drea-like, fragile gardens
where ice touched the trees and ponds

and made everything tolerably white and clean.
   Like paper whites that glow with a clear light
from the inside, though they are small and nothing

much after all. So they sat with nothing
   to say at Ryoanji garden, and a pamphlet even said
they should think of nothing, they should envision

the rocks as islands in the sea or mountaintops
   peaking above clouds.

But how is this nothing? She thought.
   And she thought of the little town she taught in
and the peaked mountain across the street from her house

and how when she was very old she might think of that mountain
   and it might grow more beautiful in memory
although it was beautiful enough as it was,

green, steep, unforgiving in its beauty.

# SOUVENIR

Seriously, she said, I want to have
a long boring talk about our relationship.
They were now drunk. Starlight streaked by.
Pachinko parlors full of madness.
She was very ill. She needed medical attention,
but what did they care it was all so blindly
full of color—blue/ red. She bought a small bowl
with a face painted in it, hell, she bought four
the death number, she would numb herself
to death, she loved another. In the morning
hung over, tremendous pain.
Two geisha outside tripped down the lane
loaded with rice cakes in banana leaves.
This is the pain, it washes on and on,
the famous dewdrop hovering on a leaf,
a man hosing the butcher shop from blood.

# THE NOTHING FLOWER

She read through her many poems about Japan.
She thought she had too many, but then here's another one.
On a hot July day, sometime in the last millennium,
her ex-boyfriend said, You act like such an authority on Japan.
You've only been here a year, what makes you the expert?
The teachers' lounge in which they were chatting
was heavily air-conditioned and she snapped back,
something nasty, no doubt because that was her way.
Later, however, his words came back to haunt her.
Actually, always his words haunt her, all his words,
like the smooth brown seeds she found and planted
thinking they were nothing,
thinking they were probably nothing special at all,
but when they grew they stretched and bloomed themselves
into unidentifiable flowers blown fragrant and nice.
Of course his words haunt even this metaphor,
as she evades everything he ever said
slipping from his well-meaning hands
to change from this metaphor to that metaphor
always a Meredith, but never the same Meredith twice.

# TIME TRAVEL MACHINE

The sky moves faster today,
I am not afraid.

The clouds are impenetrable,
their colors are different.

The sun pretends to be round,
though I know it is a different sun.

Trees, trees, trees everywhere,
and all the trees have leaves.

If I tell you about reflections,
you won't understand.

You think you know reflections,
I see future ones

reflected in reflections.

## PONIES

Past the cul-de-sac Walt kept
                    the ponies.

He bought them at the T&
                    D that once

supplied hay. We hung around,
                    felt like two

million bucks every time one
                    just looked at

us. Our mothers watched Oprah
                    and said, "That's

nice go see the ponies," while
                    handing us

popsicles shaped like missiles.
                    The ponies

took turns playing in the field
                    the Sears is

now. They were happy to live
                    not so long.

# THE FLY

Cherry blossoms loom large
on a dark tree. Girls are largely
made of cherry blossoms,
each of their dark eyes
is a weird, fully formed cherry.
Dark fly, you are part vegetable,
part mineral, part animal.
Sift vaguely in your invisible pot,
swirling atoms with your front limbs.
Your eye is like a million eyes
seeing every girl and every angle,
your eye that could be the eye of God,
your strange little eye is the eye of this poem.
Please don't fly away, don't flee,
leaving us stranded with one girl,
one angle, and no cherry tree!

# A SEAL

lives in a child's plastic pool
on Miyajima Island, Japan.
He swims back & forth—
forth on his front, back on his back—
hitting cold water out of a rusty faucet
smack on his belly. People point
him out & take a snapshot.
Miyajima boasts
mysterious pines with mist clinging
& shops with oysters & cheap handkerchiefs.
Also, the largest rice paddle in the world.
On this island, Yoshimoto wrote,
"Upsetting, but funny too,
even when my parents lay dying, I kept farting."

# NO CURRICULA

It was a lesson done all with chalk
teaching us red flowers
of an impossible variety.
She was so bossy.
Still, the flowers fell away.
Meredith broke them staring too long
and the illness was released at last.
So chalky, everyone was forced to wear a mask.
A small person can exercise control.
Even if the flowers seem real.
Even if the day is run on lesson plans.
After three months, Meredith reached the light box.
It has everything you can dream.
My god, you can teach anything there.

# LIGHT BOXES

A light box made a terrible tree.
Another shaped a home in the smoke
where the river crashed through.
The mountain, again it stood steep, green.

Ghosts could now rise
from the cemetery, high school kids
smoke through the maples, white ribbons shine
from the shrine like snakes.

Misato on the train platform
waved hello and then good-bye
and tangerine trees on the hill died,
bloomed, small white flowers

remained separate.
They turned to early snow.
Of course the train chugged
through other towns and other lives,

through tunnels echoing,
it broke many hearts.
Meredith, exhausted, remembered
every little thing, saw it happen again.

The made-up icy arrow
shot through the dark and pierced her.
This the one event light boxes
could neither predict nor record.

# RELATIONSHIPS

The lightness of many statements
And the trees were evergreen
And the children were there
The whispering was the crickets
And a tin can fell from a tree
The silence was for old people
The glittering object was the sea

# THE VIDEO GAME

The video game fit in a matchbox
surrounded by the dried pistils

of honeysuckles. It came in three colors,
and outmatched any desire.

No thing, not even bees,
could mimic its complex movements.

It sang in the hearts of children
in one size and three pixel-colors.

It led children over the White Ladies,
and through the icy pass.

It led them to the place of pistols,
and outmatched any desire.

We now know some of them
were forced to eat others of their kind.

# MEREDITH

Before I could be certain
of what they made,

and what they made in me
and called my life,

I was released,
let to live again,

rabbit streaking through the snow,
splotch of fire, a vixen foe,

my keeper shouting,
*Don't go, don't go*

# O-BON

The man fishing pulls something in
Cool and black and slippery

Night, soon the festival begins
My bike light glows feebly

Lights the moss covered tunnel
Water seeps in

The swallows, done
Cicadas, done

Still, heat and gnats
All night, these circling thoughts

You like a ghost to me
My chest blown through

A lasting
Place in the cemetery grass
Where deer slept in dew

## RELATIONSHIPS

The first time he hit her it was a mistake.
She said she'd buy the groceries.
She said Jesus then you buy the groceries.
There were so many aisles.
Cans on sale but not all cans.
A checker wouldn't give cash back
Over one hundred bucks.
He said it wasn't his deal.
Then on the highway
She alone with him, as they say, forever.
Stars as many as there ever were and less.
Headlights picked up the sign:
Only 28 miles to the Trees of Mystery.

# AT THE HOME OF THE FAMOUS POTTER

Celadon pots stacked high made lovely
glistening columns not dissimilar
to those belonging
to temples of dynasties past.
The man had made pots for sixty-seven years.
What do you have to say for yourself,
he asked. A vase looked like an opaque gray
flower, it went through the fire
and looked less so. It gained its dew.
In the manner of the mentally ill, she said,
you are ruining my life. It was more
impressive than words, just as
some dynasties are reduced to their pottery.
Though she thought she knew the truth,
even through fire,
or perhaps because of that fire,
dynasties continue to be made of people.

## ANEMONE

Some survive a thousand years.
See the moon circle, the stars

and sun, too. Waves grow and peel away.
Little nubs push up

and fall away. Some thing,
only a brief reflection in the tide pool,

only a quivering shadow,
is me,

and the other part,
seemingly nicer and more

unseemly growing from my shoulder,
is you peering over. The anemone,

having no head of its own to speak of,
grabs at our modern faces

reflected on the water. Its tentacles
clasp or grasp, though by now

we are hidden behind this page.
The anemone's feathery green

fronds tangle
with the eye of the poem

which has been all along
manipulating the ocean and the world.

# GENETIC GIANT

It was a pony, the smallest pony alive,
No bigger than an aspirin,
In fact, one could hardly spy
It from afar one had to come this close.

Of course it couldn't be caught.
Its tiniest sweat was stars.
Pony stepping everywhere twice
And nickering about the mosses.

Listen! The pony led Meredith
Far beyond Accounts Payable or Receivable.
It revealed the Cascades in Winter
As she'd seen them as a child—

Pink and orange in the first light,
Before the eastern stars began to fail.
You had to be this far to see then all,
Giant and small, vivid and pale.

There was a book on sheep I loved to hear and wouldn't let my father read another. It was a shabbily ordinary story and my father worked on banning it from our house forever. "Wouldn't you like to hear," he asked, "the story of a magic cup, or a fairy, or a withering witch down a deep well?" I only wanted that regular sheep penned in a brown barn by a creek, and the farmer carding her white wool, boiling it like clouds in a light sky, dying the fine white blue. How the wool spun round and round on a wheel—growing thinner, longer. My father worked from nine to five selling fish on the telephone. He wore ties specked with roosters, and brought home cakes glossed with "Meredith!" in cursive. Soon I could read myself to sleep, under posters of exotic lands, and my whistling father—grown gray with cancer—brought me quartered apples for my bad skin. But the sheep. The sheep stayed the same age. It rolled on its simple industry. It had its slow life apart from me. My father dreamt of a regular sheep penned in a brown barn by a creek. Its white breath in winter made a circle around the first snowfall in December. Even the soft suggestion of a different life went round on a wheel stopping only once to change hands.

# THE MIST CARRIAGE

There was a baby once,
but she is lost.
She was pulled from the soft down,
she was a whisper pulling herself

down the white wings
of a Honolulu hospital,
cleanly through the terra cotta halls
that gardenia and gardenia.

There is a bridge on the way.
Orange lights reflect on Great Auntie,
on Grandma, on the lake, man-made.
They are Japanese, who will Mother be?

My sister and I know.
In the dark Chevy, they hand us
sugar violets, pale flowers
iced in their layer of snow.

# SHADOW BOX

The rabbit
pawed dark prints
in the thickening snow.

Sweeping the roof
of the shrine still strung
with white ribbons of summer,

the father of the father
of the chemistry teacher
caused the rabbit

to startle. Surely
some of the time I did not
think of you,

paw prints pressed,
and less and less.

# FOR THE ARCHITECT

Your eyes are cast shadows.
You understand form
by the shadow
it makes, you make the form
with a shadow in mind.
Outside
almost edible greens,
a white funnel gathers water
in perfect ingenuity.
You turn to me in our cold bed.
Turn my shadow out,
the limitless plant. Gold bug.
Leaf, and drain.
Turning the poem hardly matters now
the rain, the rain.

# BIRD OF PARADISE

The aunt and the mother
led the funeral procession after the hearse
and the cars with the pall bearers
in their rental car.
No, no that's not the way,
the aunt and the mother
cried to the hearse
and took the other road.
No, no, they waved to the procession
not that way, but the procession
proceeded without them.
The mother was sure she was going
the right way and wondered
how the hearse would ever find the grave,
she was sure it would rain.
Somehow, though,
their shiny red car driving alone
against the green side of Punchbowl
met the hearse
and joined the line of other rental cars,
sliding back into place so easily
it was as if they had never parted.
As if every relative
in every rental car
was not a tourist, as if the cars
were their own
to steer
wherever they wanted,
an inheritance, a snaking dynasty
made of traps,
an eternity
made of bodies.

# ORANGE BLOSSOMS

She walked
the orange farmers' road
up through the bamboo-covered hills
past the temple
where high school kids
smoked weed and where no
bamboo trees grew
there were orange trees
white in bloom
and sweet. Farmers sprayed the leaves
with DDT and the strong
scent of orange flowers seemed deadly
even to breathe. She walked
this road every day in June
because she had an urge and
thought all the way of home
and how things would be
when she returned to it.
And every day the scent
kept coming and a little rain dripping—
and even today dripping—
from petal to leaf to dirt
and through to the clear creek
which ran its ancient path
down the hill
to be the too-sweet water,
the drink of the now forgotten town.

# NOTES

"O-bon"— O-bon is a Japanese Buddhist custom to honor the deceased. During this time, a period of several days in August, the spirits of ancestors are said to revisit household altars.

Both "Space Needle" and "Hot Air Balloon" are inspired by "Man and Derailment" by Dan Chiasson.

"The Light Box"— The line "Beauty is everlasting and dust is for time" is from Marianne Moore's poem "In Distrust of Merits."

## ABOUT THE AUTHOR

**MEREDITH COLE** was raised in Redmond, Washington and received a Masters of Fine Arts in Poetry, as well as a Masters in Teaching, from the University of Washington. Her first collection, *Miniatures*, was the winner of the 2011 Marsh Hawk Press Poetry Prize.

Meredith's poetry has appeared in *Poetry*, *The Iowa Review*, *Field*, *The Seattle Review*, *Poetry Northwest*, and other publications. As an elementary school teacher, she works to impart her passion for literacy to children. From 1999–2000, she taught English in Uwajima, Japan. Currently, she teaches the fourth grade in Seattle, where she lives with her husband and son.

# Titles From Marsh Hawk Press

Jane Augustine, *A Woman's Guide to Mountain Climbing, Night Lights, Arbor Vitae*

Sigman Byrd, *Under the Wanderer's Star*

Patricia Carlin, *Quantum Jitters, Original Green*

Claudia Carlson, *The Elephant House*

Meredith Cole, *Miniatures*

Neil de la Flor, *Almost Dorothy*

Chard deNiord, *Sharp Golden Thorn*

Sharon Dolin, *Serious Pink*

Steve Fellner, *The Weary World Rejoices, Blind Date with Cavafy*

Thomas Fink, *Peace Conference, Clarity and Other Poems, After Taxes, Gossip: A Book of Poems*

Norman Finkelstein, *Inside the Ghost Factory, Passing Over*

Edward Foster, *The Beginning of Sorrows, What He Ought To Know, Mahrem: Things Men Should Do for Men*

Paolo Javier, *The Feeling Is Actual*

Burt Kimmelman, *Somehow*

Burt Kimmelman and Fred Caruso, *The Pond at Cape May Point*

Basil King, *77 Beasts: Basil King's Bestiary, Mirage*

Martha King, *Imperfect Fit*

Phillip Lopate, *At the End of the Day: Selected Poems and An Introductory Essay*

Mary Mackey, *Sugar Zone, Breaking the Fever*

Sandy McIntosh, *Ernesta, in the Style of the Flamenco, Forty-Nine Guaranteed Ways to Escape Death, The After-Death History of My Mother, Between Earth and Sky*

Stephen Paul Miller, *There's Only One God and You're Not It, Fort Dad, The Bee Flies in May, Skinny Eighth Avenue*

Daniel Morris, *If Not for the Courage, Bryce Passage*

Sharon Olinka, *The Good City*

Justin Petropoulos, *Eminent Domain*

Paul Pines, *Last Call at the Tin Palace*

Jacquelyn Pope, *Watermark*

Karin Randolph, *Either She Was*

Rochelle Ratner, *Ben Casey Days, Balancing Acts, House and Home*

Michael Rerick, *In Ways Impossible to Fold*

Corrine Robins, *Facing It: New and Selected Poems, Today's Menu, One Thousand Years*

Eileen R. Tabios, *The Thorn Rosary: Selected Prose Poems and New (1998-2010), The Light Sang As It Left Your Eyes: Our Autobiography, I Take Thee, English, for My Beloved, Reproductions of the Empty Flagpole*

Eileen R. Tabios and j/j hastain, *the relational elations of ORPHANED ALGEBRA*

Susan Terris, *Natural Defenses*

Madeline Tiger, *Birds of Sorrow and Joy*

Harriet Zinnes, *Weather Is Whether, Light Light or the Curvature of the Earth, Whither Nonstopping, Drawing on the Wall*

For more information, please go to: http://www.marshhawkpress.org.